KU-540-013

# Cub Camps
# and
# Pack Holidays

The Scout Association
25 Buckingham Palace Road
London SW1W OPY

# Cub Camps and Pack Holidays

Compiled by:
**Hazel Addis**
**Desmond Baker**

Editors:
**Audrey Milan**
**Valerie Peters**

General Editor:
**Ron Jeffries**

Illustration:
**Peter Harrison**

Design:
**David Goodman**

Copyright © 1972
The Scout Association

SBN 85165 027 9

First Edition
First Impression
June 1972

Second Impression
September 1972

Printed in England by
Kent Paper Company Ltd, London and Ashford, Kent

# Contents

# Introduction

One of the most enjoyable and worthwhile activities in Cub-Scouting is a Pack Holiday. Like all worthwhile things it is a good deal more demanding than the ordinary weekly meetings, and equally more rewarding.

The advantages of a good Pack Holiday – and there should be no such thing as a bad one! – are tremendous. But before the Cub Scout Leader becomes swamped with his own enthusiasm, much less that of his boys, he must face up to the work and the responsibilities involved, and he should establish a clear picture of his aims and objects and the priorities which must never be lost to sight.

The emphasis should be on the word 'holiday', which suggests a complete change of scene and way of life, and a lot of fun and enjoyment in good company and healthy surroundings. A Pack Holiday however is still Cub Scouting, indeed it may be a vital part of the Pack programme, providing an opportunity for all the excitement, adventure and practical activities which Cub Scouts need. It will probably be the highlight of the year; a never-to-be-forgotten time.

For the Cub Scout Leader it provides a unique opportunity to get to know the individual boys better than ever before; to widen their interests, advance their training and to make them more self-reliant and dependable.

Another important object of a good Pack Holiday, whether based on a permanent building or under canvas, is to give the boys an even keener appetite for Scouting and the greater adventure of a Scout Camp.

There is nothing new about these aims and objects: they are the basis of Cubbing, common to all Cub Scout Leaders. But here is a method by which they may be implemented in an extensive and wholly delightful way.

# Policy,
# Organisation and Rules

These are the Rules of The Scout Association which apply to Pack Holidays. Keeping the rules is essential in order that your Pack Holiday may be covered by The Scout Association Insurance Policy.

The Rules concerning Pack Holidays are shown in *Policy, Organisation and Rules Parts 1, 2 and 3,* Appendix VIII — Activities, Rules and Instructions:—

| | |
|---:|:---|
| Camping Standards | 1, 2, 3, 4 |
| Visits Abroad | 5 (i) |
| Cub Scouts — Pack Holidays | 6 (i, ii, iii) |
| Cub Scout Camps | 7 (i–v) |
| Hostels | 8 (i–ii) |

# Chapter 1

# A Pack Holiday or a Cub Camp?

As soon as a Cub Scout Leader starts to be attracted to the idea of a Pack Holiday, there are two important decisions which must be made before all other considerations:
1. To go or not to go.
2. To sleep in a building or under canvas.

## Responsibility.

The Leader of a Pack Holiday really has to undertake enormous responsibilities and these must be faced. He will be solely responsible:

(a) **For the Cub Scouts** who will be dependent on his arrangements for their health, comfort and enjoyment.

(b) **To the Parents** who are entrusting the Leader with the safety and welfare of their children, both physically and morally.

(c) **To The Movement.** That the Pack Holiday will in no way discredit The Scout Association in the eyes of the public and of those who are good enough to hire or lend their premises and land to us.

These are very great responsibilities, not to be undertaken lightly even by the most experienced Leader. They are not merely a matter of commonsense, nor can the problems be fully understood by reading books or attending courses. Experience as an assistant on a well-run Pack Holiday is essential training for the Leader. But that experience should *never* be bought at the expense of the happiness, comfort and safety of the Cub Scouts.

The Rules governing these points must be studied and most strictly kept. They are not written just to make life difficult but are the fruits of experience and are absolutely necessary, both for guidance and as safeguards.

On the other hand, and weighing up the responsibilities against the opportunities, a well-run Pack Holiday can have a very good effect on all these people to whom we are responsible; on the boys, by providing them with the fun and adventure which they expect of Cub Scouting; on the parents, who gain a better understanding of our work, and are often more willing to co-operate as a result; and on the public, whose sympathy and support is often enlisted after they have seen for themselves the infectious happiness and good manners of a Cub Scout Pack on holiday.

Pack Holidays are optional and valuable as they may be, if any Cub Scout Leader does not feel equal to the responsibility, planning and work involved, it is much better for him to be honest, face up to the fact and decide against taking his Pack away. Maybe he needs more experience before he is ready to undertake such a project – more equipment, better facilities or more qualified helpers. Whatever the reason, it is right to reject the temptation before the Cubs know that it exists.

Having decided that you are going to organise a holiday the next important decision is should it be a Pack Holiday or a Cub Camp? You will of course be guided by your own experience, the advice of others and the facilities available.

## Types of Pack Holidays.
### EITHER
The Cub Scouts are based on a permanent building for their sleeping accommodation
### OR
The Cubs sleep in tents, some form of alternative accommodation being available in wet weather. This is generally known as a Cub Scout Camp.

In either case cooking may be done indoors or out of doors –

camp style, and the programmes of activities for the Cubs will be much the same, so too, the responsibilities and pre-planning. You should first refer to the Rules concerning each type of holiday (*Policy, Organisation and Rules, Parts 1, 2 and 3*, Appendix VIII. Rules 6 and 7). Then weigh up the pros and cons in general and in particular as they apply to you and your Pack.

**Pack Holidays based on a building have these special advantages:**

(a) They are more insulated against the weather. Our British Summers do have a habit of producing a series of 'deep depressions' which are apt to lower the spirits of boys sleeping under canvas for the first time, and might prejudice them against camping in the future. It is easier to keep bedding dry and equipment stored in a building, and to dry wet garments.

(b) There is less preliminary work for the Leaders and Advance Party in collecting and checking camp equipment, erecting tents, making latrines and planning the layout of camp. It is possible too that the Troop may be needing their camping equipment at the same time.

(c) Many Leaders find it less of a challenge indoors, to provide the necessary services and care, especially if they have not had a great deal of experience in camp themselves. If camping, they would have the added responsibility of safeguarding the Group's valuable camping equipment.

(d) For a boy's first experience of a holiday away from home it may seem more secure, if a little less exciting, to sleep in a building.

(e) The whole Pack may go on a Pack Holiday of this type, whereas only boys over nine years six months are allowed to go to a Cub Camp. This makes it possible for a Pack to go on holiday where the average age is rather low. But the Leader is of course free to make his own decisions about an age limit (in either case) and about the best number of boys to take. This, in turn, may be governed by the number of staff available and the size of the accommodation.

(f) This type of holiday makes it possible for a country Pack to spend their Pack Holiday in a town, which may be just the adventure and fun that they would most enjoy.

## Pack Holidays in Camp also have special advantages:

(a) It is much more adventurous to a small boy to sleep in a tent and indeed most Cub Scouts say they would prefer this kind of Pack Holiday.

(b) It is often easier to find privacy and beautiful surroundings – which Cubs do appreciate.

(c) It can give confidence, in anticipation of Scouting, always providing that it is a really well-run Camp and the boy is taught the elementary rules of making himself comfortable.

(d) The spaciousness and freedom are relaxing and undoubtedly help a boy who suffers from restrictions and frustrations at home. This is, of course, particularly true of town boys who may have little opportunity for country holidays.

So there is a great deal to consider and each Leader must decide for himself which type of Pack Holiday is best suited to his own Pack, the facilities and the finances available.

You should discuss the idea with other people, seek advice and take advantage of the experience of other Scouters. Particularly that of your Group Scout Leader who should be concerned with your planning from the very beginning and whose permission you must have. The Assistant District Commissioner (Cub Scouts) will probably have had considerable experience of both sorts of Pack Holidays as will the District Commissioner, from whom you must have written permission in the early stages of your planning.

**Two other possibilities present themselves:**

(a) **A Pack Holiday in a Hostel** belonging to some other Organisation. See *Policy, Organisation and Rules, Parts 1, 2 and 3,* Appendix VIII, Rule 8, with its important clauses.

(b) **Joint Holidays.** This does not mean combined camps of Scouts and Cubs, which is generally discouraged and can only be done under special circumstances with the District Commissioner's permission. A Joint Holiday is one in which two or three Packs combine, with the most experienced Leader in charge. This plan has advantages for a small Pack with an inexperienced Leader, who might otherwise be unable to take his Pack on holiday. It is also economical in food, equipment and pooling of staff and their experience. The disadvantages are a certain loss of family spirit because the Pack is not entirely on its own. The Leaders don't know all the boys and vice versa. It is possible that other Packs may not seem to have quite the same standard. These points call for a great deal of thought and the Leader may decide that he should be the only one to go, and so start his apprenticeship.

Chapter 2
# Preparation 1 -
## First Steps

The whole success of a Pack Holiday depends on planning and the amount of time which is given to making proper preparations.

## Records.
From the very beginning it is wise to keep a notebook, recording all data and decisions, facts and figures as well as a file for all relevant correspondence. This will serve as an invaluable reminder and reference, and will be a tremendous help in organising future holidays.

The headings in your notebook should include the following subjects, as far as possible in order of priority, although you will find that many decisions are dependent on one another.

## Group Scout Leader's Approval.
This should be obtained before you commit yourself in any way. The Group Scout Leader will need to be certain that you are properly qualified to lead the type of Pack Holiday that you have chosen.

## Qualifications.
You must be the holder of a Pack Holiday Certificate, which is obtained by attending a Pack Holiday Course.

But the first requirement is to have helped on a Pack Holiday run by a qualified Scouter. If you are going to take the boys to camp, then it is necessary that you should have assisted at a Cub Camp: and have your Pack Holiday Certificate endorsed to this effect by the District Commissioner.

It is the Group Scout Leader who will assure the District Commissioner that you match up to these requirements and it is the District Commissioner who has to give the final permission at least two months ahead of the date of the project. The Group Scout Leader who, of course, knows his Leaders well, should also be satisfied that you have the right character for the undertaking. The task of organising a Pack Holiday calls for a lot of patience, stability and stamina as well as enthusiasm and it may be that all these qualities are going to be highly tested. Undoubtedly, the exuberance of the Cubs will be rather wearing, but their obvious enjoyment is always adequate compensation.

## Staff.

(a) **Numbers.** The rule is that there must be at least one adult for every six Cub Scouts, excluding the Leader in charge of the holiday. Also that three adults is the minimum, two of whom must be Leaders in the Movement, and one of those must hold (or have held) a Warrant in the Cub Scout Section.

This is the bare minimum and you may well decide that you want more than this when you come to consider the allocation of jobs, the specialist duties and the need for reserves, or people who are able to serve in a dual capacity in the event of someone falling out.

(b) **Sources.** Obviously your first choice will be your own Assistant Cub Scouters. You are already a team, used to working together, you know the boys and they know you. But you will probably need more help than that. Scouters from other Sections in the Group might enjoy the opportunity to work and play with the Pack, and their 'know-how' would be invaluable, especially if you are going to camp. The Group Scout Leader is the ideal person, and if he can't be there the whole time he will certainly try to visit you. Cub Scout Instructors would be extremely useful members of the staff. Patrol Leaders can be of help, if the Scout Leader agrees and if they are not already committed to their own Section. Venture Scouts may be pleased to be asked for help and this could form part of the 'Service' requirement of the Venture Scout Award Scheme. Parents or friends too might be invited to help with specific jobs.

The important thing is that those people whom you select for your staff should be able to work together as a harmonious team. Choosing the right people calls for a great deal of thought and maybe tact on the part of the Leader.

Where there is a mixed staff, you will of course have to make provision for separate sleeping and toilet accommodation.

Although we are used to working with Scouters of both sexes, the public are always prone to gain the wrong impression and to judge the Movement by one misunderstanding; so we must be seen strictly to observe the conventions.

The team once selected, should have regular meetings in order to get to know each other better and to evolve detailed plans. These decisions together with the allocation of duties should be listed and everybody should have a copy.

In some cases it may be an advantage to have a trial weekend together, because 'you have to live with folk to know 'em'. This may be especially useful if your holiday is going to be under canvas and some of the staff may have had no experience of camp, although it must be remembered that a camp without boys is a very different thing to the rigours of a Pack Holiday.

1. **Special Duties.** The Scouter in charge of the holiday is responsible for general supervision and co-ordination and should not undertake 'specialist duties'. You will need a few specially skilled members of your staff.

2. **Catering and Cooking.** One expert is needed, who can estimate quantities and qualities of vitamin value. He or she should know something about a small boy's taste and powers of consumption. He should also be able to provide a properly balanced diet and cook the food in the conditions available. He will need at least one experienced assistant and relief cook. Between them, they undertake the whole of the catering, menus, shopping, store-keeping and supplies, cooking and 'domestic economy'. The help of Venture Scouts would be invaluable here. This obviously calls for experience and a great deal of preparation. If supplementary stores are to be used, these too need a practical hand.

3. **First Aid, Health and Hygiene.** One person should be a competent First Aider who could cope with any emergency until qualified medical help could be obtained. He or she should be able to deal with minor accidents and ailments, which are common to children especially when they are away from home. This person would be responsible for the 'Sick Bay' – separate accommodation, which must be reserved purely for First Aid use – and for supplying the First Aid Box and being responsible for its contents.

Again, in the event of accident or illness, help might be needed from some other 'dual capacity' member of the staff, with some knowledge of First Aid and/or nursing. One of these two people should also be responsible for Hygiene, including the disposal of refuse, sanitation, ablutions and rules of hygiene, such as washing hands after using the toilets, drying wet clothes, airing bedding, etc.

4. **Programmes and Activities.** These of course will be the responsibility of the Cub Scout Leader. Some camping experience and knowledge of places of local interest will be of

value, as well as the capacity to deal with a wide range of Cub Scout Arrow work, wide games and special activities.

*Note:*— Some of these duties inevitably overlap, which calls for plenty of good pre-planning in detail, co-operation, give and take — and good leadership.

There will also be other jobs to allocate:— quartermaster, treasurer, tuck shop, wood and water. If you are camping you will need a lot of experienced help. Always remember, however, if you have with you Scouters or Patrol Leaders from the Troop, that this is a Cub Scout Holiday which is entirely different from a Scout Camp.

Some Cubs too may want to help and all members of the staff should be ready to encourage them to undertake smaller responsibilities and chores. They enjoy collecting wood, carrying water and even, strangely enough, doing the washing-up. It is all part of the fun. If they are allowed to cook at least one meal for themselves, even if it is only bangers in a frying pan, it will be the best they ever tasted. All this suggests that the minimum requirement of three adults on the staff would only apply to the smallest number of boys on holiday and would, in fact, be very inadequate.

## Sites.

In making enquiries and searching for a suitable site, you should take these important factors into consideration:

(a) You do not want to be too far away from home, especially for your first Pack Holiday. The boys only want a complete change of conditions, without too much travelling involved. In case of sudden illness or even acute homesickness, it will be a help to be within easy reach of home.

(b) If it is to be a Pack Holiday based on a building, the accommodation and facilities must be adequate for all your requirements, or easily augmented.

(c) If the Cubs are to sleep in tents, the site must lend itself to a proper layout for camp, with enough level ground for tents and games; wood and water available and a good permanent shelter — which could be a marquee, if there is room for it and if your funds are equal to it. Suggestions for possible sites may be gleaned from many sources. You will be wise to mention the project to plenty of people. Headquarters publishes a list of camp sites, although some of these sites are not always suitable for Cub Scouts. There is also a list of undesirable sites — *Restricted Areas for Camp Sites.* But probably your local enquiries will be more fruitful, especially in search of a permanent building for a Pack Holiday.

1. **Types of Buildings:** (a) Group headquarters – some of these, particularly the newer ones, may be suitable. But, as with all other people's property, you will have to be very careful not to do any damage; or, if there is any, you should see that it is suitably repaired or replaced.

(b) Schools, Youth Centres, Village Halls or Community Centres, Headquarters of other organisations such as Women's Institutes – all these can prove suitable accommodation. Those that are sited in towns may provide a rural Pack with just the right centre they need for a change of surroundings. Hostels of other organisations, including the Youth Hostel's Association, can provide most excellent facilities, provided they can meet the requirements of our Rules. These are given in *Policy, Organisation and Rules, Parts 1, 2 and 3,* Appendix VIII, Rule 8. The rules of the establishment and the provision of meals could be a great relief to an inexperienced Cub Scout Leader.

(c) Farm buildings and outbuildings – these need to be treated with some caution. Few of them are as clean and quiet as we should like. Any of these buildings might also prove suitable as the permanent shelter which is an obligation for Cub Camps, provided that they are within easy reach of the camp site.

2. **Accommodation for sleeping indoors:–** ideally you will need:

(a) A good clean, airy, watertight building, big enough to house the numbers you propose to take, not forgetting the staff, although some of these may be able to sleep in tents.

(b) Suitable sleeping arrangements. Smaller bedrooms to take about six boys means that they will settle down more quickly than in a dormitory. Enough beds or bunks, or space for air or camp beds on the floor. Separate sleeping accommodation is needed for the staff, with special consideration for the comfort of those who are not Scouters. Everybody should be able to enjoy the holiday!

(c) Adequate toilet facilities. One lavatory to ten Cub Scouts and one wash bowl to three people is considered to be about right. If there are insufficient lavatories you may be able to supplement them with chemical lavatories such as Elsans or Racasans providing these are under cover.

(d) Good cooking facilities, able to provide for your numbers, and a good sink. Also dry, clean food storage. A separate dining room is desirable, if possible..

(e) Services. Electricity or gas, for lighting, cooking and heating, remembering the possibility of having to dry clothes. If the water supply is not piped mains water, it may be necessary to check its source and, possibly, to consult the local Water Board. Fire hazards and the need for supplementary fire precautions should also be considered.

(f) One room large enough for indoor activities if wet.

(g) Equipment. List what is available, in the way of chairs and tables, as well as beds and bedding, cooking equipment, crockery, etc, in order to estimate what else you must bring.

3. **Camp Sites:–** here, your first consideration should be:

(a) Drainage – avoiding clay for waste disposal; or low lying muddy areas.

(b) Space for layout of tents and level ground for play area.

(c) Water – close to hand, plentiful and safe for drinking.

(d) Aspect – giving protection from prevailing wind, but not too near trees, especially elms which are apt to shed quite heavy branches without warning. Although a sunny aspect is delightful, some shade should be available.

(e) Fuel – if you are dependent on wood for cooking fires, this should be close at hand; it must be suitable for burning and you must, of course, have permission to use it.

(f) The permanent shelter for wet weather – big enough and

reasonably close. As this is an obligation for Cub Camps it may well be a deciding factor.

4. **Further Considerations for both types of Pack Holiday:**– the most attractive sites and desirable accommodation may have to be relinquished if they do not match up to the final list of requirements:

(a) Ease of access – for delivery of equipment and boys.

(b) Privacy – you do not want to be invaded by the public, or by farm animals. Your boundaries and theirs must be clearly established.

(c) Availability – on the other hand you will want to be within reasonable reach of shops, a farm or other sources of supply; early closing day should be noted. A telephone should certainly be within easy reach, and you should make a note of the whereabouts of the nearest doctor.

(d) Natural Assets – attractive surroundings are important and a view is appreciated by Cub Scouts. Ideally you should find a stretch of open country or moorland, some woodlands, a stream or the sea within easy reach. Also places of local interest are a help to your programme planning. All these will add to the boys' sense of excitement and adventure, and lend themselves to outdoor Cub Scouting activities.

(e) Natural hazards – should be considered at the same time and it is best to avoid sites which offer too many opportunities to accident-prone Cubs; such as cliffs, railways cuttings, busy main roads, deep rivers or dangerous bathing. If any bathing is to be included in your programme, you will be well advised to study the rules in advance. (Ref. *Policy, Organisation and Rules, Parts 1, 2 and 3,* Appendix VIII, Rules 34 to 37).

(f) Dates – check when the site or accommodation will be available. If other people are using it before you, you will want to be certain when they will be out of it and, incidentally, that it will be left in good order.

(g) Fees – establish a clear understanding with the owner of exactly what the charges are and what they will include in the way of water, lighting and equipment. Both these latter points should be kept in writing, in your file.

5. **Preliminary Visits:**– it is essential for a Leader to visit any possible site for a preliminary inspection. Promising sites may call for two or three visits and on later occasions you might be wise to take some of your staff with you. This would be a

great help to your cook and programme planners in making their preparations.

6. **Check List:–** apart from recording all these points in your notebook, perhaps one heading per page, in order that you may augment them from time to time, it is a good plan to have a duplicated check list, which you can take with you when prospecting for a site. There are so many things to be remembered and a collection of ticks or crosses on your list may help you to make an earlier decision. Here is a sample check list as a summary to this chapter, but you may prefer to compile one of your own, having decided on your priorities and the special needs of your Pack.

---

**Pack Holiday – Check List:**

O.S. Map Sheet: ....................................................

Grid Ref.: ............................................................

Place: ................................................................

..............................................................

Date of preliminary visit: ........................................

Name and address of owner/caretaker:......................

..............................................................

..............................................................

..............................................................

Telephone number: ...............................................

Travelling time: ....................................................

Cost: ................................................................

Distance from home: .............................................

**For Indoors:** A plan of the building (size of rooms etc.)

Accommodation: ....................................................

Facilities: (lighting, toilets, cooking, etc.) ...................

..............................................................

Equipment provided: (chairs, tables, beds, bedding, utensils, etc.) ............................................................

..............................................................

..............................................................

..............................................................

Outdoor space: ....................................................

---

**For Camp:** A plan of the camp site (water, wood, marshy ground, etc.)

Access: ...........................................................

Space: ...........................................................

Flat Ground: ...................................................

Water: ...........................................................

Aspect: ..........................................................

Wood: ............................................................

Soil: .............................................................

Natural screening: ............................................

...................................................................

...................................................................

**For Either:** Nearest shops: ............................

...................................................................

...................................................................

Early closing: ..................................................

Nearest telephone at: .......................................

Telephone No: .................................................

Doctor: ..........................................................

...................................................................

Telephone No: .................................................

Church/Chapel: ................................................

Garage: .........................................................

...................................................................

Telephone No: .................................................

Local attractions: .............................................

Local hazards: .................................................

Other notes:

...................................................................

...................................................................

...................................................................

...................................................................

...................................................................

...................................................................

...................................................................

...................................................................

...................................................................

...................................................................

...................................................................

...................................................................

...................................................................

...................................................................

...................................................................

...................................................................

...................................................................

# Chapter 3

# Preparation 2 -
## Next Steps

So far we have only grappled with the question of the site, staff and the first essentials. There is still a lot to consider in the way of preparation.

## 1. Date and Duration.

The season for Pack Holidays with the best chance of good weather is May to September. If the plan is for a mid-week holiday it must obviously be during the school holidays and must not clash with too many family holiday arrangements. Generally speaking Bank Holidays are not a good time for week-end Pack Holidays because of the difficulty of travelling. Parents should be notified as early as possible.

Pack Holidays should not be too long, especially for the first venture. A week-end, or a long week-end from Friday to Tuesday, is quite enough to start with and a week should be the maximum.

In the case of Cub Camps it may be felt that such a short period scarcely justifies all the extra work in assembling tents and the extra equipment, but even then, four to five days is quite enough and a week still the absolute maximum.

## 2. Costs.

These will take quite a lot working out and your staff should be involved in discussing them. The cook should be able to produce menus and estimate the cost of food, to which should be added the charges for transport, any hiring fees and the cost of extra equipment, and camp fees. Parents should be told approximately what it is going to cost them, at the first notification. In addition to this costing, it is wise to provide a safety margin in case of emergencies and the unforeseen.

## 3. Transport

Arrangements for transport need to be made at an early stage. You may find that one member of your staff is willing to undertake the responsibility for this, if you discuss it at a staff meeting. As you will only be going a short distance from home, rail travel will probably be unnecessary, although you may get special rates for parties, if you should need it. The cost of transport from the station to the site has to be off-set against this.

Equipment will probably need to go by lorry, but this is not very good for the Cubs themselves. It is much better to use a motor coach, and the costs are much the same. In both cases it is wise to check that they are properly covered by insurance.

Most Groups can usually find private transport, if the Group Committee, parents and supporters are asked to help, and this is usually the safest, cheapest and quickest method. Private vans are particularly useful, but again insurance should be checked.

## 4. Permits:–

The District Commissioner's permission comes in two stages.

(a) **Preliminary Consent** must be given in writing before any definite arrangements are made and before the Cub Scouts or their parents are told anything about it. This must be at least two months before the date of the proposed holiday, and in some cases the District Commissioner may require three months. (See *Policy, Organisation and Rules, Parts 1, 2 and 3*, Appendix VIII, Rule 6 (i).)

(b) **Final Approval** for which the Leader must apply at least twenty-eight days before the event. For this he submits a completed 'Permission to Camp' form (P.C. (Cub Scouts) ), together with the Registration Fee of 25p.

The District Commissioner is responsible for ensuring that all equipment, including tents, if they are to be used, is inspected beforehand by a Leader experienced in Cub Scout Camps, and this Leader must be someone other than the Scouter in charge. He will also need to see your programme for wet or dry weather. He will not give his permission unless he is completely satisfied with the leadership, equipment, accommodation and site. So obviously the more information you can give him the better it will be. Tell him of your own qualifications and your arrangements for your helpers, parents, transport and other plans.

The District Commissioner's written permission together with any other correspondence, should of course be kept in your file. Also the written permission from the owner of the site, when you have definitely booked the accommodation and paid any deposit.

## 5. Numbers:–

It is best not to take too many Cubs, especially if this is your first venture. With a big Pack it might be wise to take only Sixers and Seconds for a trial week-end holiday, although it will involve just as much care and preparation and would only economise in quantities of equipment and numbers of staff.

Although you are allowed to take Cubs of any age on a Pack Holiday based on indoor sleeping accommodation, it doesn't mean that you must take the whole Pack. Equally, although nine years, six months is the minimum age for Cubs going to camp under canvas, it does not necessarily follow that you must take all the Cubs above that age.

It is up to you and your staff to decide on the purpose of your Pack Holiday, whether it is something specific such as Badge work or Nature Study, or perhaps it is just for fun. Then you should decide on the maximum number to achieve the purpose and with which you can cope in the accommodation available. Having decided on your age limit, or other qualifications, you must, of course, stick to the rule and make no exceptions.

## 6. Notification to Parents:–

This should be done well in advance, say six weeks before the event, as you will have to tell the District Commissioner that you have the parents' permission.

An immense amount of tact is needed here, as you have to decide first which boys and how many you are going to take on the holiday (guided of course by the nine years, six months age rule) but not let any of them know of the possibility until you have their parents' consent. The excitement is going to be tremendous, but if anything goes wrong the disappointment will be even greater.

You may like to call a parents' meeting to discuss the project in detail with those parents who are concerned, but you cannot send the notice calling a meeting by way of the sons, who are not meant to know anything about it! If it is to be a small-sized Pack Holiday, you would probably be wiser to visit the parents individually in their homes. Many Mums would find it easier to discuss personal details in private, while some with small children are not free to attend a meeting.

You should also consider the boys and their parents who have not been chosen to go on the holiday. They should be helped to understand the reason. If there is a fixed age limit, or perhaps an Arrow standard, this will avoid any feelings of discrimination.

The Cubs who are too young will of course look forward to next year, so perhaps you should beware of making rash promises. Pack Holidays are not an annual obligation, although you may well become an addict!

The co-operation of the parents is of great importance. They will want to know all about your plans: when, where, how and details about the care and welfare of their sons. If it is to be a camp they will need reassurance about arrangements for reasonable comfort and wet weather. If there is to be a visiting day this can be planned, although for a short week-end it will probably not be considered necessary. They should be told of the cost per head and given a list of the equipment each boy must take.

In return you will want to know any particulars about diet or medicine for their sons, including the possibility of bed-wetting, which is not uncommon in boys of Cub Scout age. In such cases a waterproof sheet ought to be added to the list. If you decide it is best to call a parents' meeting you will need to circulate a letter, together with the list of equipment and a form of permission for the parent to sign.

Here is an example of such a letter, to show what sort of information should be included.

........................ *Cub Scout Pack*
*Cub Scout Leader's address and*
*telephone number.*

*Dear ..................,*

*We are proposing to hold a Pack Holiday from .........*
*............ until ................... and hope that you will allow your boy to come.*

*This will be held at .........................................*
*and the boys will sleep in .......................................*

*The cost of the holiday will be £......... and I should be grateful if you would pay the deposit by ...............*
*(date). Transport will be by ..................., the cost being included in the above figure.*

*A meeting will be held at ............... on ...............*
*to explain all the arrangements and I hope that you will be able to come to discuss details.*

*In order that we may know which boys will be coming, I should be pleased if you would sign the permission form at the bottom of this letter. We will collect these slips at the meeting, or, if more convenient, I will gladly come and visit you.*

*I also enclose a list of equipment your son will need, but please consult me if you have some difficulty about any of these items.*

*Yours sincerely,*

*Cub Scout Leader.*

### Parents' Permission Form.

Please delete as necessary and sign:

I agree that .......................... may/may not attend the Pack Holiday to be held on ...........................

Signed: ..................

Please return this form to the Cub Scout Leader by: ...............................

**Personal Equipment.** Before they give their consent, parents will want to know what they are letting themselves in for, as some of the kit required might prove quite an expensive matter. It might be possible to borrow some items, like ground sheets or sleeping bags, from the Troop, but some parents may need help in this respect.

A list, based on the following suggestions, should be duplicated and issued with the letter of notification and permission form.

**Equipment List:** The following is a list of the kit, in addition to full uniform, your boy will need to take with him on the Pack Holiday.

## Please note that all articles should be clearly marked with his name.

*Kitbag, rucsac or holdall.*
*Groundsheet.*
*Air or camp bed – if desired.*
*Sleeping bag with 1/3 blankets plus 6 blanket pins or at least 4 blankets plus 12 blanket pins.*
*Air pillow or old pillow case.*
*Pyjamas.*
*Raincoat, anorak or plastic mackintosh.*
*Plimsolls or sandals.*
*Wellington boots.*
*Old shirt and shorts.*
*Spare long-sleeved jersey.*
*Spare pair of socks and change of underclothes (in polythene bag).*
*Handkerchiefs.*
*Towels.*
*Soap, flannel, toothbrush and paste (in plastic bag).*
*Comb.*
*2 plastic plates (one deep one).*
*Mug – plastic or other unbreakable material.*
*Knife, fork and two spoons (one teaspoon and one desert spoon) in a plastic bag.*

Swimming trunks.
Torch.
Pencil or ball-point pen.
Card game, book or comic if desired.
Stamped addressed envelope (if the holiday is longer than a week-end).

## NOTE: NO pocket knives please.

*It is best that all boys should have approximately the same amount of spending money and we suggest that they should bring no more than ..................*
*The kit should be brought to ...........................................*
*at .............................. on ..............................*
*The boys will meet in full uniforms at ................................*
*(place) on .............................. (date) at ........... (time).*
*They should arrive back at .............................. (place) on*
*........................ (date) at .............*
*Please let me know if you have difficulty in obtaining any of the above items of equipment.*
*(Signed)...............................*

**Health Form.** When you know which boys are going on holiday with you, it is you who will need some reassurance about their health, any allergies or physical peculiarities which you may not know about already. Although it is best to discuss this with parents in a friendly way -- perhaps over a cup of tea laid on after a parents' meeting – it is necessary to have it in writing, *duly signed by the parent. Forms such as the following example* should be duplicated, explained and issued, with a fixed date for their return.

*.............................. CUB SCOUT PACK*
*Dear ..................,*
*Before taking your boy on the Pack Holiday on*
*............ I should be glad if you would let me know:*
*Does your son have to take any medicine or pills?.........*
*(If so they should be clearly marked with his name and the exact dose, and handed to me before departure).*
*Is there any food he must not eat? ..............................*
*Does he suffer from any allergy or disability such as: travel-sickness, asthma or bed-wetting? ........................*
*(If so please advise about precautions or remedies).*
*....................................................................................*
*....................................................................................*
*May he bathe under careful supervision? ..................*

*Has he had an anti-tetanus injection within the last six years? ...................*

*Has he been in contact with any infectious disease during the last three weeks? ...................*

*In the event of an emergency, are you willing that he should have an anaesthetic? ...................*

*Please state his National Health Number ...................*

*and name of the Family Doctor ...................*

*Please return this form, giving all the above information by ...................*

*Parent's signature ...................     Date...................*

**Note:** It is safest for the Leader in charge of First Aid to keep any medicine or even laxatives which the parents may send, and to issue them to the boy as directed.

## 7. Equipment.

Apart from each boy's personal kit, you have to decide and list the equipment you will need for general use on the Holiday. This is dealt with in the next chapter.

## 8. Preparing the Cub Scouts.

When you have received permission from the District Commissioner and your other arrangements are well in hand, the moment comes when you can break the news to the boys.

You must explain how many or how few are going, why the limitation and how you have fixed it. The excitement – also the inevitable disappointment of some – can be used as a training incentive. Anticipation, whether it is for this year or some future occasion, is all part of the fun and you will be bombarded with questions.

For the next week or so your Pack programme might include some special preparatory training, such as:

Making their own beds with blanket pins;

Packing and care of kit;

Proper use of groundsheets;

Proper use of latrines (if they are to be used);

General rules of hygiene;

If a camp, special tips for care of the tents;

If in the country, a little of the Country Code, and an appetiser for outdoor activities.

If in town, a little preparation in the way of items of local interest or history and the Highway Code.

The fact that the Law of the Holiday will be the Cub Scout Law.

If any Cub shows any doubt or reluctance to go, it will be wise to discuss this privately with his parents and not to press him unduly or allow the other boys to jeer.

## 9. Advance Party.

This should consist of yourself and as many volunteers from your staff, or volunteers by persuasion, as may seem necessary for the preliminary work which you have listed.

Their job is to make the immediate preparations so that everything is ready to swing into operation, the moment the Pack arrives.

(a) For a Holiday based on a permanent building, there is probably a Caretaker, with whom you should already have made friends and shown your willingness to co-operate; in return for which you may expect the place to be open, aired and clean. You will be bringing supplementary equipment to be sorted out, installed and erected, as well as extra tables, chairs, bedding, kitchen gear and crockery as necessary. You may have to erect:– tents for extra accommodation for staff or for stores; outdoor fireplace and incinerator; additional chemical toilets indoors, or outdoor latrines if necessary; a flagstaff, etc.

Stores or other deliveries, ordered in advance, must be checked by a member of the cook's staff, the kitchen prepared and either a hot meal ready for the boys, or at least a hot drink. This will depend on the length of the journey, and the time of arrival; remembering that this might be in bad weather and that first impressions are important. The Cubs will want to unpack their own kit, even if it is delivered in advance, and make their own beds.

(b) For Cub Camps the Advance Party will have more to do and will need more time to do it, in order to have everything absolutely ready and in the sort of order in which you want it to be kept. This will apply to sleeping tents and First Aid and Store Tents; the kitchen with all its layout, refuse disposal and incinerator; latrines, dining shelter, camp fire circle, flagstaff. You must not forget any arrangements needed in the permanent shelter, and if this is a marquee it takes both time and skill to erect.

You will no doubt have decided on the best layout on a previous visit to the site and it would be a good idea to have copies of the plan for each of your assistants.

You will, of course, compile a list of your Advance Party, noting their special allocation of work and the times when they will be arriving on the site.

They should also be prepared to constitute a 'Rear Party', as there will be a lot of clearing up to do after the boys have gone: final packing up of equipment, returning any gear borrowed locally, filling in latrines and pits, and generally leaving the ground in as good, if not better order than you found it.

## 10. Camp Layout.

Note some of the important features:

(a) The tents should be arranged in a semi-circle, opening towards the South, slope permitting, the Scouters' tent or tents in a good position to keep an eye on all that goes on. Tents for Lady Cub Scouters, close to their own latrines and ablutions, and far enough away to give them some privacy. The boys' tents near enough to each other to make them feel within calling distance, but not too near.

(b) The flag staff will normally be in a central position to one side of the open area and the camp fire some distance away, if possible in a picturesque setting.

Here would be an ideal layout:

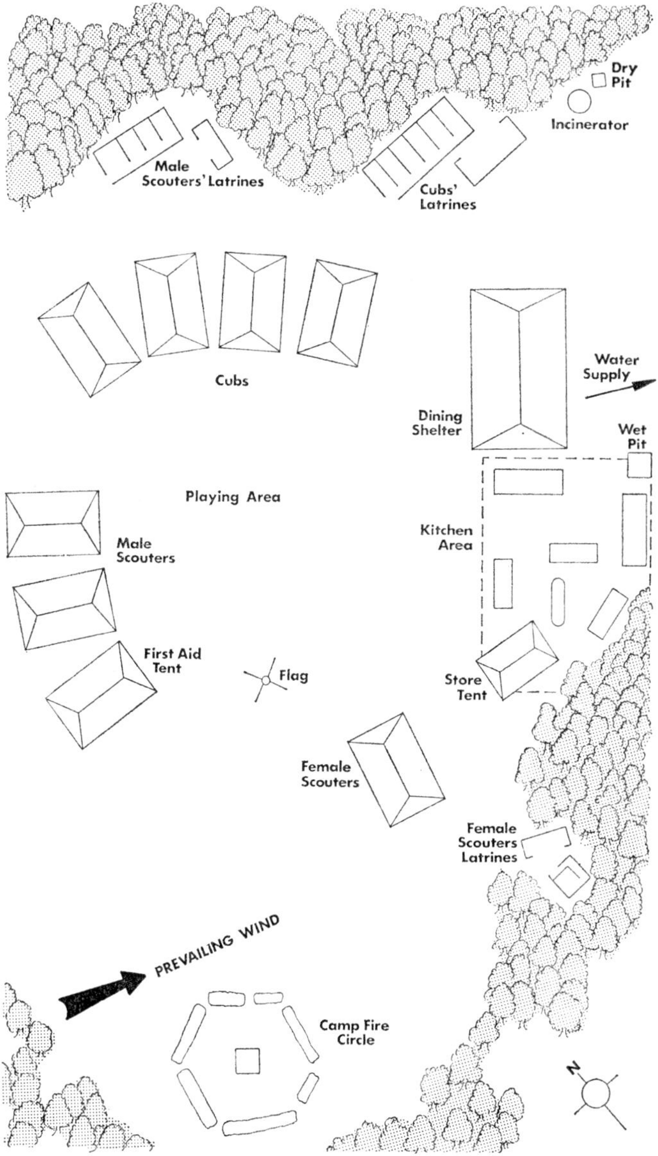

Dry Pit

Incinerator

Male Scouters' Latrines

Cubs' Latrines

Cubs

Water Supply

Dining Shelter

Wet Pit

Playing Area

Kitchen Area

Male Scouters

First Aid Tent

Flag

Store Tent

Female Scouters

Female Scouters Latrines

PREVAILING WIND

Camp Fire Circle

N

33

c) The prevailing wind must be considered and the kitchen sited so that smoke will not blow into camp. It should be as near the water supply as possible.

(d) Wet pits should be close by the kitchen on the far side from the tents. Incinerator further away down wind, together with the dry pit, which can also take ashes.

(e) Store tent in the kitchen area, up wind of the camp.

(f)   Dining shelter also near the kitchen and up wind.

(g) The washing place needs to be near the water, though not necessarily the drinking water. If possible it is a good plan to site the washing place between the latrines and the camp.

(h) The First Aid tent or Sick Bay should be away from the boys' tent but close to one of the Scouters' tents.

(i) The latrines need a sheltered place down wind of the camp, at a reasonable distance but not too far away from the boys' tents.

# Chapter 4

# Equipment

It is the Leader's responsibility to list the equipment required and to arrange for its supply, taking into consideration:

What is already on the site.

What the Group can provide.

What can be obtained locally (on hire or possibly on loan).

What each boy will bring.

What each member of the staff will bring in addition to their personal kit. A duplicated list will avoid any confusion. The 'specialist' members of the Staff will no doubt help to compile a list of their own special requirements.

## Equipment for a Pack Holiday.

The whole list, formidable as it seems, may be broken down under these headings:

(a) **Indoors:** Any additional beds, chairs, tables, utensils, washing bowls, etc;

Chemical toilets with fluid (if necessary), disinfectant.

Any extra crockery, cutlery, etc.

**NOTE:** If cooking or feeding out-of-doors see reference to camp kitchens and dining shelters, below.

(b) **General, for both types of Pack Holiday:**

Tents, for accommodation, Sick Bay, stores, as necessary.

Union Flag, Flag Staff, or pulley and halyards.

Spare groundsheets.

Rope, string, sisal.

Boxes or plastic bags for litter.

Soap, towels, toilet paper.

Shoe cleaning outfit.

Good supply of swabs, mops, drying-up cloths.

Washing-up liquid, scouring pads, scrubbing brush.

Emergency lighting:– lanterns, torches, matches.

Tools:– entrenching tool, spades (at least two).

Activity equipment:– gear for games, football, tennis balls, bean bags, cricket things, etc.

Wet weather activities, dressing-up gear.

Bible, prayer book, hymn sheets or books for use at Scouts' Own Service.

**(c) Sick Bay:** (whether indoors or in a separate tent)
>Bed, spare blankets, pillow.
>Kettle, pressure or gas stove.
>Hot water bottle.
>Chamber pot, bowl, jug, mug, towel.
>Torch or lantern and matches.
>First Aid equipment and medicine chest.

# For Cub Camps (extra to above).

(a) **Tents:** complete with poles, pegs, mallets, ground sheets.
(b) **Dining shelter:** screening or overhead protection, trestle tables, benches or planks and supports, plastic table cloths.
(c) **Latrines:** screening for latrines and wash-house, with poles and overhead shelter. Buckets, wash-bowls and stands, lantern, toilet paper containers, towels.
(d) **Extra tools as required:** Rake, digging fork, pick-axe, bush saw.
(e) **Camp Kitchen:** Material for building altar fire; supplementary cooking stoves, appropriate fuel; 2 tables or boxes (for kitchen and store tent); 2 tressel tables; supply of boxes and tins or plastic food-containers and polythene bags; at least 2 lanterns; matches; supply of butter muslin; pudding cloths; 2 large plastic tablecloths.
(f) **Cooking utensils:** (figures based on a camp for 16 Cubs and 4 adults)
>*4 large dixies (at least);*
>*4 small dixies;*
>*2 large frying pans;*
>*6 large metal bowls for mixing or storing (one may serve for a roasting bowl if desired);*
>*3 large plastic bowls for washing-up, cleaning vegetables, etc.;*
>*3 large enamel or plastic jugs;*
>*3 large plates;*
>*2 mugs, pint or half-pint for measuring, etc.;*
>*2 large ladles;*
>*1 milk can with lid (unless bottled milk can be delivered daily);*
>*1 butter container;*
>*1 tin opener;*
>*Supply of knives, forks, spoons (including carving knife and fork and wooden spoon).*

Note: Choose utensils that are easy to use and easy to clean.

Plastic plates and mugs are better than chipped enamel.
However small in numbers the Pack Holiday may be, it will be found that all these items of equipment are necessary. The Leader should not risk the comfort of the boys or staff, or indeed the success of the holiday, by mistaken economies.
You are more likely to add to the list, especially with such personal requirements as notebooks, log book, cash box or bag, repair outfits, torch and spare batteries.

## Tents.

Remembering that this may be a Cub Scout's first experience of sleeping under canvas, we must do all we can to make it a reasonably comfortable, safe and enjoyable holiday.
Tents should be in first class condition. Ridge and frame tents are the most suitable, providing the maximum headroom. Cubs and their belongings take up more space than you might imagine and it is quite enough to have five boys to one Patrol-size tent (approximately 3m. x 2$\frac{1}{3}$m. x 2m. (9ft. x 7ft. x 6ft.) with a metre (3ft.) brailing).
A fly sheet is important, giving added protection against the weather.
Without a fly sheet it is important not to touch the canvas from the inside during rain, and this is not an art that Cubs learn quickly.
Brailings should be rolled up during the day and tied with a slip reef, which is easier to release in a sudden rainstorm. If the sod cloth is wet in the morning, the brailings should be looped outwards to dry off.
Tents should never be completely closed at night, if doors are pegged outwards they will usually give enough protection from wind and rain.
One overall groundsheet is best for Cubs, or individual groundsheets should be laid to overlap, if possible.
The tension of canvas is affected by sun and dew, wind and rain. Canvas and guy lines should be kept taut, sagging canvas causes undue strain, while flapping canvas may tear in a gale.
A member of the staff should be responsible for the care of the tents, for slackening guy lines off at night and tightening them in the morning.
Tents are by far the most expensive part of camp equipment, and the Cubs should be taught to look after them. This is especially important if the weather is wet and the sleeping quarters have to be kept dry and free from mud.

# Equipment

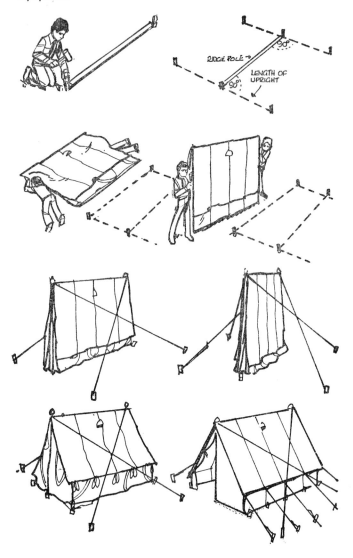

Pitching and striking tents is a job for the Advance and Rear Parties, as all tents need to be erected before the Pack arrives, and they are the last thing to be packed up before departure.

Chapter 5

# Health and Hygiene

The Cub Scouters are responsible for the health and welfare of the boys while on holiday, and high standards of hygiene are necessary in order to ensure this.

Both the parents and the owners of the property will take a dim view of Scouting in general if your particular group lowers the standard.

## 1. Toilets

**A holiday based on a building** will probably have proper indoor lavatories, or, if not, well-constructed outdoor ones under cover and close at hand. If the existing arrangements have to be supplemented (the ratio being a minimum of one lavatory to ten boys), the chemical closets are the best, or, if not available, buckets with seats. In this case an adult member of the staff must be responsible for emptying them daily into a properly sited pit. Such buckets must be clearly marked.

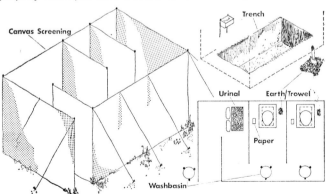

In camp you will probably have to construct latrines. These trenches should be approximately 1 metre (3ft.) long by ⅓m. (1ft.) across and ⅔m. (2ft.) deep, over which some form of seating arrangement can be constructed. There should also be a separate urinal, a small trench or pit, ⅔m. (2ft.) deep, and lined with pebbles.

The Cubs will want some instruction in the proper use of these, and the rule about shovelling a little earth after use. A pile of fine earth, a trowel and toilet paper in a water proof container must be supplied. For the latter a tin with a lid or a jam jar hanging horizontally above ground level is the best.

There must also be a firm camp rule about washing hands after using the lavatories. This rule should also apply to indoor lavatories, and is one of the habits we should like to cultivate in Cubs at all times.

For Cub Scouts a latrine tent is ideal if rather expensive, but some sort of strong screening with overhead cover is essential. Some privacy is desirable, too, if it is only a 'Vacant' or a 'House Full' notice. It should be made easy for the boys to use the latrines whenever they wish, and from this aspect they must be clean and reasonably comfortable. If they are kept in proper order there will be no unpleasant smell and no need to use disinfectant. At night a lantern should be left burning outside the latrines, or night buckets may be supplied nearer the tents. Some boys are more afraid of the dark than they will admit.

When about half-full the latrines must be filled in firmly, the site marked as foul ground with a cross of sticks and new trenches dug. Space should be allotted for this in the original layout. Fresh urinals may have to be dug, too, if the original ones cease to drain properly – some sanitary fluid may have to be used.

It must be a regular job for an adult to inspect latrines, to make sure they are kept in good condition, and to decide when it is time to make new ones.

Toilets for Leaders must, of course, be entirely separate and should be made as comfortable as possible.


## 2. Ablutions.

**With indoor accommodation** these should be quite straightforward, though again they may need supplementing with plastic bowls, as the ratio should be one bowl to three people. **In camp** the washing place should have some screening, and some sort of bench or stand made for the bowls, with duckboarding to stand on, if possible. There should be a sump, well away from the area, for the disposal of waste water.

The boys should not keep their towels or washing things among their kit; arrangements should be made in the wash-house for soap and flannel, toothbrush and paste. There should be a line for towels, indoors and another outside on which to dry them when it is fine.

Again an adult must be responsible for the wash-house, both to see that it is used and kept in order.

## 3. Disposal of Refuse.

A Pack Holiday is a wonderful opportunity for teaching the boys practical habits of cleanliness and tidiness. Plans for the disposal of all types of waste should be included in the original layout, prepared by the Advance Party before the Cubs arrive. For the digging of pits you must have the permission and advice of the owner of the site.

**Solids.** Whichever type of holiday it is, you may be able to have the use of a dustbin, but all burnable rubbish should be burnt in an incinerator. These are quite simple to construct — two types are illustrated here — and should be sited down wind of the camp.

Where stoves are used for cooking rather than open fires, a 'burn-all' is essential.

From the beginning tidiness should be a rule of the Holiday, and the Leaders need to set a scrupulous example by never dropping litter or leaving gear lying about. There should be plenty of litter boxes or bags hanging in accessible places, the contents of which have to be burned regularly. This is an opportunity to teach Cubs something of the Country Code and the courtesy due to property owners.

Tins should be burned in the incinerator (to avoid attracting flies), bashed (so that they take less space and are less dangerous), and should be disposed of later. If not they should be gathered together for the refuse collector. Note that aerosol and similar containers must not be burnt as they explode when heated.

Plastic bags can constitute a danger both to young children and to animals if left lying about in the country. They must be disposed of by burning or taking them home.

**Liquid Waste.** With indoor plumbing care must be taken not to block the drains with too much greasy water or tea leaves. It is safer to construct a wet pit outside.

In camp it is desirable to have a wet pit with grease trap, but you should check that the owner has no objection to the digging of pits. This consists of a hole about the size of a large bucket (not sited on clay soil) with a good layer of cinders or small stones at the bottom. The opening is covered with a lacework of brushwood, which again is covered with coarse grass. This trap holds the grease and particles of food, so that only liquid is poured into the pit and soaks away, while the trap is burnt and renewed twice daily.

## 4. First Aid.

You are bound to have a few small upsets and minor ailments to deal with, if not possibly some emergencies. Cub Scouts are of the age to be somewhat 'accident-prone' and, although we certainly mustn't molly-coddle them or fuss unduly, precautions have to be taken to avoid accidents or hazards to health, and preparations made for a qualified person to be able to deal with such troubles.

(a) A First Aid room or tent which must be fitted up ready for immediate use, and should not be used for any other purpose. This must be in the charge of an experienced person, qualified to deal with First Aid and children's ailments. The necessary contents of the Sick Bay are listed on Page 36.

(b) Contact a local doctor, who should be informed in writing before the Pack arrives and given exact directions on how to reach the site. His name and telephone number should be displayed in the Sick Bay, and the staff must not hesitate to seek his advice if worried or in any emergency.

## 5. Health.

The boys themselves should be encouraged to report any cuts and scratches for treatment. If they are 'off colour' it is usually pretty obvious and up to the Cub Scouters to try and discover the cause. This may be due to homesickness, apprehension, over-excitement and subsequent exhaustion, or to the change of diet or drinking water. In such cases, rest, quiet and re-assurance will probably be all the treatment that is needed,

but if the upset persists, with diarrhoea, vomiting or pain a doctor should be consulted.

Camp kit should be sensibly adapted to suit the occasion. Bathing trunks should be worn for football in the rain, plimsolls or wellingtons for early morning dew and a pullover in the evening or after swimming, before the boys feel chilly. If they do get wet, a good rub down followed by a change of clothing, will safeguard them.

A rest hour after the midday meal is a good idea, when the Cubs may read or play quiet games – this is important for all concerned.

A Pack Holiday is a good opportunity to put into practice your indoor training on hygiene and healthy habits, more especially the germ warfare against dirt and flies.

## 6. Sleeping.

Sleeping bags are a great asset and simplify the business of bedmaking, although blankets are usually needed as well. The boys must be warm to ensure a good night's sleep. Cubs should be shown how to make up their own blankets with blanket pins, and the proper use of groundsheets stressed. These should be checked by an adult before 'lights out'. Special precautions must be taken with sleeping bags if there is any danger of bed-wetting.

Air-beds are excellent, especially for indoor sleeping, where floor-boards are extremely hard and existing mattresses may be damp. In camp, air-beds are optional of course, though some Cubs might think it far more fun to sleep on the bare groundsheet.

Boys must not be allowed to wear their underclothes at night as these need airing. Pyjamas should be worn next to the skin, though a pullover may be worn on top if necessary.

The first night in either type of Pack Holiday is apt to be a little restless to begin with, but thereafter it should be understood that 'lights out' is a rule to be observed, for everybody's sake. A child of Cub Scout age needs ten hours sleep.

The Cub Scouters should also remember that having insisted on quiet from the boys they should not create too much of a noise themselves.

# Chapter 6

# Catering
# And Cooking

*'Good food badly cooked is no longer good food'*

The task of catering and cooking for a Pack Holiday is a very important one, and calls for a person with practical experience of dealing with fairly large numbers.

Useful books are 'The Scouts' Cook Book' (7½p) and 'A.B.C. of Cookery' (25p), both available from the Scout Shop.

The Leader should be able to rely on his cook to draw up his or her own list of requirements and to bring or order the necessary supplies, and to take proper care of the kitchen, whether indoors or outside.

In order to make preparations in good time, the cook will need to know as early as possible.

1. The approximate numbers of boys and staff.
2. Any diets or allergies, as stated by parents and any religious obligations.
3. The boys' likes and dislikes, before making plans, though normal meals satisfy all but the most particular.

4. The names and addresses of local tradesmen and suppliers, and if and when they will deliver. Also early closing day, which should have been checked on a preliminary visit.

# 1. Catering.

The aim is to provide a well-balanced diet, with plenty of fresh meat, vegetables and fruit and avoiding too much stodgy food. Some knowledge of food values and vitamins is important:

### 1. For body-building:

Calcium for teeth and bones:– milk and cheese.
Protein for flesh and muscle:– milk, cheese, fish, eggs, peas, beans, lentils, nuts.
Iron for the blood:– liver, egg-yolks, vegetables, meat, dried fruit.

### 2. For energy and warmth:

Carbohydrates:– Fats and fatty food.
Sugar:– Starchy food.
(More of these are needed in cold weather than hot).

### 3. For protection:

Food containing vitamins to keep the body in good condition.

**Vitamin A.** For growth, healthy skin, throat, lungs, eyes.
– contained in liver, butter, milk, carrots, leaf vegetables.

**Vitamin B.** For healthy digestion and nervous system.
– contained in cereals, brown bread, milk, lean bacon, liver, pork, eggs, peas, beans, potatoes.

**Vitamin C.** For healthy skin and general well-being.
– in fruit and vegetables, particularly oranges, lemons, grapefruit, blackcurrants, tomatoes, potatoes, leaf vegetables and salads.

**Vitamin D.** Adding to the calcium for bones and teeth.
– fish, liver, margarine, egg yolk. And lots of sunshine!
Note: That natural vitamins in food are easily lost in cooking. For instance vegetables should be cooked in very little water, and the water that is left should be used for making gravy, as it contains the valuable vitamins. 'Variety is the spice of life' and it is also important to health. It is helpful if the cook is able to adapt the menu to suit the weather and the day's programme. The Cub Scout Leader will decide whether to have the 'big' meal at mid-day or in the evening.

# 2. Ordering.

It is often wiser to buy by number rather than weight, e.g. 32 sausages for 16 boys, rather than so many pounds. Bacon rashers, tomatoes and fruit can usually be bought this way, too.

With ready-sliced bread you will know the number of slices per loaf, or it can be cut to your requirements.

Sugar in 2lb. packets and fats in half-pounds are easier to handle than bulk amounts. Many firms are helpful in supplying catering sizes of tinned and packaged food. Their help and advice is well worth enlisting.

Duplicate copies of orders should be made, and checked on delivery.

It is also wise to keep in your log book a copy of all orders and menus with a note beside each stating amount of excess or under ordering, and the costs involved, for use on another occasion.

## 3. Storage.

All food must be kept covered against dust and insects. You should take a plentiful supply of aluminium foil, butter muslin, plastic food containers and polythene bags (to keep vegetables fresh).

It is worth taking a metal meat safe, into which food can be packed for transport so that it will not take up valuable space.

All food containers except for unopened tins and vegetables should be raised off the ground.

Soap, paraffin or any form of disinfectant should be kept well apart from the food, and the bottles or containers clearly marked.

Milk containers should stand in a pail of water and be covered with damp butter muslin, with the corners hanging in the water.

Butter containers may be kept in the same way, but the damp muslin should not touch the butter – there should be no direct contact, as bluebottles can lay their eggs through the muslin. If attacked by ants all containers should stand in bowls of water, or the legs of a table may be placed in saucers of water.

In camp even greater care should be taken to safeguard food from marauding animals. A tree larder may be the best method or good strong storage boxes.

## 4. Kitchens.

**Indoors** there may be adequate cooking facilities, or supplementary heating may have to be provided in the form of a pressure stove or gas cooker. If paraffin stoves are used special fire precautions should be taken, and paraffin containers clearly marked.

In the case of a Village Hall where there is only one electric boiler or gas ring, an outdoor kitchen as for camp will probably have to be constructed.

**In camp** the kitchen must be carefully sited, as near as possible to the water supply, down wind of the main camp and on level ground. A fire shelter is essential.

An altar fire is strongly recommended, with again a supplementary stove on a firm standing and screened from draught. It is an advantage to have a tin oven to keep food hot and a camp kettle or a large dixie with a constant supply of hot water for washing-up standing on the edge of the fire, or better still a separate small fire to provide constant hot water.

The layout of the kitchen must be carefully considered, streamlining the work as far as possible.

Fence off the working area, only cooks and fire tenders allowed inside.

Cut, split and graded wood fed from sawing area, outside the kitchen area, to the covered wood store.

The altar fire must not be too high and the platform big enough to allow for an area at the side of the fire on which to rest hot dixies. The fire should be stoked regularly.

The kitchen as a whole should be arranged so that the prevailing wind takes away odours from the wet pit and smoke from the fire, without crossing the working areas.

The serving table should be arranged so that the Cubs can obtain the food without entering the kitchen area. It may be used for washing-up (drainage to wet pit if necessary).

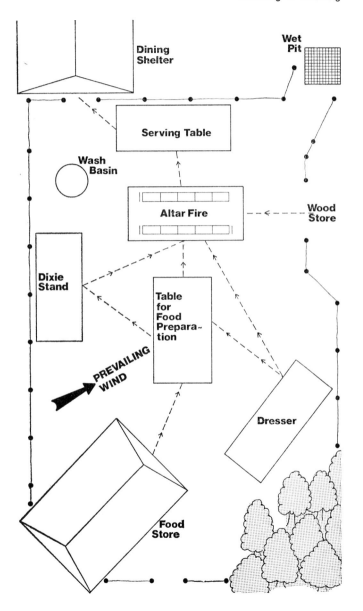

Provision should be made for covering the preparation table, fire and serving table in wet weather.


## 5. The Fire.

The type of wood used for a cooking fire is very important and below is a list of suitable and not-so-suitable woods and their characteristics.

*Tinder:* Fir cones, birch bark, dry leaves from hedge bottoms.

*Quick, hot flame:* Generally soft woods, e.g. pine.

*Hot, lasting embers:* Generally hard woods, e.g. oak.

*Burns well green:* Ash, blackthorn, holly.

*General purposes:* Birch.

*Not suitable:* Alder, elm.

*Collecting:* Dead branches from trees break off easily and if the bark is peeled are quite dry even in wet weather. Dead wood from the ground, in the climate of the United Kingdom, is usually very wet.

*Splitting:* Split wood ignites quicker than wood in the round.

*Tools:* A small bow saw is quicker, safer and more economical than an axe for cutting lengths.

*Note:* Have an ample supply of cut fuel at hand before lighting the fire.


Characteristics of some of the commoner woods:

| Type | Splitting | Burning |
|------|-----------|---------|
| Alder | Difficult | Unsuitable. |
| Ash | Very easy | Burns well, green or seasoned. |
| Beech | Easy | Very good for all purposes. |
| Birch | Very easy | Gives a good heat. |
| Blackthorn | Easy | Very good, green or seasoned. |
| Elder | Very easy | Little heat. |
| Elm | Fairly easy | Very poor when green. |
| Firs | Very easy | Quickly, with hot flame. |
| Hawthorn | Difficult | Spits dangerously, good heat. |
| Hazel | Easy | Burns steadily. |
| Holly | Easy | Good, green or seasoned. |
| Horse Chestnut | Moderate | Not good. |
| Lime | Very easy | Very poor. |
| Oak | Difficult | Slow, good heat. |
| Poplars | Easy | Poor. |
| Sycamore | Easy | Mixed with other woods gives good heat. |

## 6. Kitchen Hygiene.

An even higher standard of hygiene should operate in camp kitchens. All utensils and cutlery must be kept scrupulously clean, including the hands of anybody working in the kitchen. For this reason it is best if the cook does not have to handle the fuel.

Only authorised helpers, having first washed their hands, should be allowed inside the kitchen area. **Nobody** with a cold or with cuts on their hands should work in the preparing of food.

After infinite care in washing-up, a dirty dish-cloth may undo all the good work. It is best to use disposable cloths.

Cubs helping to clean vegetables and to wash up should know why these rules have to be followed.

**Note:** The kitchen should be arranged for a flow of work with minimum movement: e.g. Food from store – to preparing table – to fire – to serving table. Cooking equipment (dixies, ladles, etc.) from dresser – to either fire or preparing table.

## 7. Feeding.

Eating out of doors is half the fun of a Pack Holiday, where-ever the boys may be sleeping, but this should not mean a series of haphazard picnics. Meals should not be eaten in any accommodation used for sleeping. A dining shelter should be erected, with overhead protection and proper tables and seating. Meals should be properly and punctually served, with hot plates for hot meals, adequate cutlery and a plastic tablecloth.

Grace should be said (or sung) before meals, and a code of manners established from the start – hands always washed before meals and dirty plates cleared, etc.

| | Breakfast | Lunch | Tea | Supper |
|---|---|---|---|---|
| *Friday* | | | | Sausages and mash<br>Bread and Butter<br>Fresh fruit<br>Fruit juice |
| *Saturday* | Cornflakes<br>Scrambled Eggs and Toast<br>Bread and Butter<br>Tea or milk | Luncheon Meat<br>Lettuce and Tomatoes<br>Bread and Butter<br>Fruit pies | Cake or buns<br>Bread and Butter and Jam<br>Tea or milk<br>Orange juice | Liver and Bacon<br>Potatoes and Cabbage<br>Stewed fruit and custard |
| *Sunday* | Cornflakes<br>Bacon and Tomatoes<br>etc. | Veal and Ham pie (sliced)<br>Salad<br>Bread and Butter<br>Fresh fruit | 'as before | Stewed steak<br>Carrots and onions<br>Potatoes<br>Prunes and custard |
| *Monday* | Cornflakes<br>Baked Beans and Toast<br>etc. | Cheese rolls (picnic)<br>Tomatoes<br>Fruit – fruit cake | as before | Mince and dumplings<br>Carrots and onions (garnish)<br>Cabbage and potatoes<br>Peaches and custard |
| *Tuesday* | Cornflakes<br>Egg and Bacon<br>etc. | Cold Ham<br>Salad<br>Crisps<br>Bread and Butter<br>Fruit | | |

# List of stores required for Cub Camp menu: 4 days – 16 Cubs – 4 Adults – Cost £2 per head

### Dairy Produce:

¾ pint of milk per head per day.

100 rashers of bacon (easier to buy by nos. of rashers).

1 lb. butter per day.

42 eggs – this allows for breakages.

1½ lb. lard for frying.

2½ lb. cheese – this allows for some Cubs who do not like meat and for late-night sandwiches for adults.

### Meat:

3 oz. meat per head per day – this allows for varying appetites and includes: liver, mince, stewing steak – both the last two may be tinned.

Luncheon meat, cold ham, veal and ham pie – these should be bought by the slice, allowing 1 slice of pie and 2 slices of cold meat per head.

40 sausages.

### Vegetables:

100 medium sized tomatoes.

Lettuce – depends on size and kind – 2 leaves per person per meal.

Cabbage – as above but 1 large cabbage will serve approx. 10.

Carrots – 1 medium sized carrot per person – use any left over in the mince.

½ doz. large Spanish onions.

20 lb. potatoes – plus potato powder if required.

### Fruit:

40 apples.

40 oranges.

Serve fruit as it is in season with 1 lb. for every 3 Cubs.

### Bread:

Bread – medium cut sliced loaves – 4 slices per head per day.

Cake and buns – buy by the slice or individual buns (80 slices).

20 fruit pies.

**Dry and Tinned Goods:**

 2 lb. sugar per day.
 3 lb. bag of flour.
 1½ lb. suet.
 7 large pkts. cornflakes.
 ¾ lb. tea.
 2 gallons squash.
 7lb. tin of jam.
 1 pkt. crisps per Cub.
 3 oz. baked beans per head.
 8 oz. jar or tin of coffee.
 1¼ lb. drinking chocolate or cocoa.
 1 tin of custard – normal size.
 Evaporated or dried milk – normal size.
 1 pkt. salt.
 1 tin of gravy powder.
 1 drum of pepper.
 6 large tins of soup.

**Household Goods:**

 ¼ gallon of washing up liquid.
 3 pkts. scouring pads.
 3 or 4 drums of scouring powder.
 2 rolls of paper kitchen towel.
 5 rolls toilet paper.
 1 doz. boxes of matches.
 3 large bottles of disinfectant.
 6 tea towels.
 4 cloths for washing up, mopping up, etc.
 1 scrubbing brush.

# Chapter 7

# Programmes

Programme planning must be done well in advance and in consultation with those members of the staff who are specially concerned with activities.

The District Commissioner will want to see a specimen programme, with wet weather alternatives, which must be submitted to him no later than twenty-eight days before your departure date. The P.C. (Cub Scouts) Form also has this twenty-eight day stipulation.

## 1. In General.

This provides an approximate timetable and each member of the staff should have a copy of it. You must be prepared to adapt the programme to the occasion as well as to the weather. Sometimes the opportunity may occur for some unforeseen enjoyment e.g. watching the Camp Warden or Farmer fell a nearby tree, and your programme should be sufficiently elastic for everyone to be able to make the most of everything. You should know well enough what your Cubs particularly enjoy and what interests them in the way of adventurous activities.

## 2. In Particular.

Given opposite is an outline programme that is designed to show how a four day programme catering for four adults and sixteen Cubs might be arranged.

Then, in a little more detail, we have given a breakdown of some of the items shown in the programme.

We would suggest that all Cubs should be encouraged to keep a log-book of the holiday as this gives them something to occupy themselves with during the rest periods and also provides a souvenir of the Pack Holidays that they have attended.

**Saturday**

**9.45 Bronze Arrow Cubs:** Choose a tree and discover all about it, i.e. make a bark rubbing; mount a leaf under adhesive plastic sheeting; measure the tree's height and circumference; draw it's shape and the insects and birds that live in it; make a chart of everything discovered.

**Silver Arrow Cubs:** Make and set up bird feeding tables; put food on them throughout the camp; keep a log of the birds which visit them and the type of food they eat.

**Gold Arrow Cubs:** Set up a weather station, weather vane, anemometer, rain gauge, etc., and keep daily recordings throughout the camp.

Most of these activities can be carried out indoors in preparation for outdoors if the weather is wet.

**11.15. Swimming or Football:** If swimming facilities are available make use of them and try to get everyone to improve their performance or, if there are any non-swimmers, to complete the water confidence test. Organise some games suitable for playing in the water − e.g. water polo using a balloon. Ensure safety rules are kept.

Alternatively, organise football in such a way that no one is left out. Five-a-side football may be more suitable than eleven-a-side. Play can continue if the weather is wet with the boys in swimming trunks. A good rub down, a hot drink afterwards and they will come to no harm.

**13.00 Rest Hour:** Comics and books available. Work on log-books.

**14.00 Handcrafts:** Make a souvenir of the camp or a present for someone at home. e.g. Bronze Arrow Cubs: a book mark from natural materials; or a model such as a squirrel made out of pine cones.

Silver Arrow Cubs: a glider out of balsa wood; a model of the camp in polystyrene and other materials.

| Times | FRIDAY | SATURDAY | SUNDAY | MONDAY | TUESDAY |
|---|---|---|---|---|---|
| 9.45 | | Nature activities | Field games | Free Period | Free period – pack up |
| 11.05 | | Morning break | Morning break | Break | Break |
| 11.15 | | Swimming or football | Church Services | Day ramble to place | Swimming or football |
| 12.00 | | | Free period | of local interest | Lunch |
| 12.30 | | Lunch | Lunch | | |
| 12.45 | | | | | Rest period |
| 13.00 | | Rest period | Rest period | | |
| 13.45 | | | | | |
| 14.00 | | Handcrafts | Preparation for | | |
| 15.00 | | | entertainment | | Prepare to go |
| 16.00 | | Free period | Break | Free period | |
| 16.15 | | | Mini sports | | |
| 18.00 | Departure | Evening meal | Evening meal | Evening meal | Departure |
| 18.30 | | | | Finish logbooks | |
| 19.00 | Arrival at site | Science in Camp | Free period | Logbooks judged | Arrival home |
| 19.30 | Cubs explore, settle in | | Entertainment | | |
| 20.00 | Activity games | Camp Fire | | Camp fire | |

**The above programme does not include the usual morning and evening routine, which could run as follows:**

| 7.00 | Leaders rise | 8.15 | Breakfast | 20.30 | Flag and Prayers | 21.00 | Wash and prepare for bed |
|---|---|---|---|---|---|---|---|
| 7.30 | Cubs rise and wash | 9.30 | Inspection. Flag. Prayers | 20.45 | Hot drink | 21.30 | Lights out |

Gold Arrow Cubs: candle holder from a log or a key holder from wood.

These handcrafts may be done either indoors or outdoors according to the weather.

**19.00 Science in Camp:** Rig up a string telephone between tents; have a jet plane race with balloons along strings; each Six make periscopes and use them to spy on the neighbouring Six.

## Sunday

**11.15 Church Service:** Times of all local church services should be found out, any Cubs left in camp can either have a free period or field games can be organised. If it is wet the Cubs may like to put any finishing touches to the articles they made in the handcraft session on the previous day.

**13.00 Rest Hour:** Talk over ideas for the evening entertainment. A leader with each Six. After the rest hour prepare and practise items for the evening.

Suggestions for the entertainment: mime a story; make shadow puppets – using a sheet of paper for the screen, a torch for the light; give a short play; make paper bag puppets and put on a skit about the camp; do some conjuring tricks; perform songs of various types; make and use some rhythm instruments.

**16.15 Mini-Sports:** Choose events in which the non-athletic boys can participate and which they will enjoy.

e.g. egg and spoon race; three-legged race; obstacle race; throwing the hammer – a piece of string and a balloon; throwing the javelin – a drinking straw; sack race.

## Monday

**11.15 Ramble to place of local interest.** Suggested places to visit depending on the area:– castle, harbour, airport, beach, cathedral, museum.

On the way lay a trail of tracking signs (Bronze Arrow); follow a compass trail (Silver Arrow); write a song about the Country Code or (Gold Arrow) about water safety rules; follow the route on a 1in. Ordnance Survey Map (Map Reader Badge).

Take photographs of the place of interest and of the Pack (Photographer Badge).

If the area is suitable, the younger Cubs could play a wide game and the older ones could light fires and cook sausages. On the way home have an I-Spy competition.

**18.30 Finish Logbooks:** Form a panel of judges from the leaders and judge the entries. Present the prizes at Camp Fire.

**On arrival:** The Cubs should be shown round the site, the toilet arrangements explained, together with any absolutely necessary rules – the fewer and simpler the better. After that it is only reasonable to give them time to explore their new surroundings.

**Inspection:** This should be held punctually each morning, but only after plenty of time has been allowed for getting ready and using the latrines. On the first day do not expect too high a standard, but show what sort of improvements you will be looking for at the next inspection and to set things right in a friendly way, explain why we have to be particular about hygiene habits.

Indoors, beds should be stripped and the kit laid out tidily; rooms should be swept and tidied; blankets hung up to air and sleeping bags turned inside out.

In camp, kit should be laid out neatly on the boy's own groundsheet, outside the tent if fine. If the kit is arranged at one end of the groundsheet, the other is free to be pulled over the gear in the event of a shower. The overall groundsheet should also be removed to give the ground an airing. It is necessary to check that damp washing things or dirty shoes are in their right places and not concealed in the bedding.

After inspection an adult should check that there has been no bed-wetting, and do any washing or airing privately so as not to embarrass the boys in any way. One of the staff should check the tent brailings and guys, while others will be responsible for inspecting the site, latrines, wash-house, dining shelter and waste disposal.

Everyone should be in uniform above the knee after the opening ceremony, when the mode of dress for the day may be announced. Below the knees, plimsolls or wellingtons may be worn with socks, to avoid blisters, although these must be changed later if they are wet. Wellingtons should not be worn all day.

**Flag:** Some sort of flagstaff or pulley and halyards should be rigged, so that the flag may be broken and lowered with a simple ceremony each morning and evening.

**Prayers:** Following flagbreak should be short, simple and sincere. A prayer by Akela, a short Bible reading by a Sixer and a prayer for all to join in, is probably quite enough. Remember to thank God for all He has given us, which on a holiday out of doors is particularly evident, and to pray for those at home and for others who are less fortunate. Do not be afraid to ask Cubs to write their own prayers and to read them.

Evening prayers, thoughtfully chosen, should be equally brief and meaningful.

**Camp Fire:** This should be a grand climax to the day, and one of the happiest memories of the holiday. The Cubs may be allowed to help collect wood and build a pagoda-type fire. This is the safest type as it burns from the middle and falls inwards. In any case it should not be too big, and the period of the Camp Fire itself is better on the short side – say half an hour. The Cubs should sit on spare groundsheets and some proper seating is an advantage if possible.

An extensive repertoire of songs is not necessary, the majority you will need being well-known ones, with a few new ones provided they are simple to learn.

The Cubs should be encouraged to put on a few stunts, varied with some suitable games or action songs, and finishing with a yarn.

Leadership is important to allow for maximum fun and laughter but without rowdiness or ragging. There should be a formal opening ceremony, however simple, and a Prayer at the end.

It is an adult's job to stoke and control the fire and also to make sure it is out before turning in.

An indoor sing-song is the next best thing, and can provide a lot of fun.

**Scouts' Own Service:** Duty to God figures on the programme in morning and evening prayers, Grace before meals and in some special form of worship on Sunday. It may be possible to take the Pack to a nearby Church or Chapel Service, and if so it would be courteous to inform the Minister in advance. He may want to adapt his Service slightly for their benefit, especially if they are of mixed denominations. He might also appreciate an invitation to visit the site.

Alternatively a Scouts' Own Service may be arranged and can be a very happy event. The boys should be involved as much as possible, the Sixers helping the leaders to plan the programme and taking an active part in it themselves with a Bible reading or leading a Prayer. There should be plenty of singing and a suitable yarn included.

But Duty to God is not just part of the timetable: it should be an integral part of everything. A Pack Holiday may provide the best opportunity we shall ever have for helping our Cubs to realise the marvellous things that God has given us, and His love and care for us. A real appreciation of Nature and a desire to serve God by helping to share unselfishly, to show our gratitude with our lives as well as our lips, seems to come spontaneously to everybody, and the Cubs must be given every opportunity and encouragement to express this happiness.

This is largely a matter of example. It is impossible to live together in lovely surroundings without the boys reacting to our attitude, accepting our standards and noticing how each one of us lives up to our Promise. Just as we shall get to know the individual boys, better than ever before, so they will get to know us, to sense if our values are genuine, and if we practise every day what we talk about once a week at home. Everybody therefore should join in these acts of worship, with the simple reverence we expect from the boys.

## 3. Extras.

**Free time:** must be allowed, for the Cubs to enjoy themselves in their own way, without being over-organised: exploring, climbing trees or hut-building, paddling, fishing or damming a stream, 'wild beast' hunting, or whatever they most enjoy. Time too to help with some of the work, in order that they may feel they have made contributions. This to them will be part of the fun.

**Bank:** All money should be handed in on the first day for safe keeping. A careful record must be kept, and money issued daily as required.

**Tuck shop:** This is an important feature, if only to keep some check on the amount of sweets, pop, and crisps bought and eaten each day.

**Bathing and Boating:** See *Policy, Organisation and Rules Parts 1, 2 and 3 Appendix VIII.* Rules 14 to 39. **These rules are absolutely essential and must be strictly and scrupulously followed.**

# 4. Special Activities.

These, too, should have been worked out in detail, well in advance, if only so that those responsible for activities should have brought all the necessary gear.

**Outings:** On a preliminary visit you will have found out as much as you can about the local attractions and places of interest, so that you can plan expeditions. In the country these might include visits to a castle or ruins, a mill or lighthouse, an organised nature trail or even a farm, having obtained permission of course.

In town there might be a museum, fire station, railway siding or zoo.

**Outdoor Activities:** Apart from such organised expeditions, which again should be reasonably flexible, there are: wide games, scavenger hunts, treasure trails, mini sports and all the things which one never has time and space to do at ordinary Pack Meetings.

You will realise what a wide choice of activities there is if you look up the suggestions for Special Activities (Page 72), and for outdoor games (Page 132 and 133) of the *Cub Scout Leaders' Handbook.* Also the advice on running expeditions, wide games and trails on Page 79.

**Imaginative Themes:** There are the 'Special Pack Meeting' type of activities, peculiar to Cubbing, where an imaginative theme is chosen and developed into a tremendous variety of games, text badge work-in-disguise, dressing-up and all sorts of fun and nonsense. Out of doors, themes like Space travel, Robin Hood, Wild West or East African Safari may trigger off a whole afternoon of varied activities.

**Handcrafts** of a more ambitious type than those done at home, may be enjoyed indoors or out, especially if they are concerned with making things that can actually be put into use immediately: kites, catamarans (made out of washing-up liquid bottles), hot air balloons, bows and arrows, stilts, or a few simple Camp gadgets like tent hangers, mug trees, plate racks or whatever the Cubs think they need.

# 5. Indoors.

In wet weather it may be possible to adapt some of the above activities, such as mini sports, dressing-up for themes like 'A Mad-Hatter's tea-party' and of course handcrafts. There are also nature collections to be mounted and exhibited, making miniature gardens or a zoo with natural materials, potato

carving or printing, leaf-rubbings or a mini games tournament.
Some of these, together with painting and quieter games may be enjoyed during the rest hour.

To summarise: variety, the unexpected and the adventurous are the most important ingredients to successful programme planning, together with as much change as possible from the ordinary weekly activities of the Pack.

**Chapter 8**

# In Conclusion

It is a good idea for the staff to get together after a short lapse of time to assess the whole project. Having had the chance to sort out their impressions and to get things into perspective, everybody should be encouraged to express their feelings and to make suggestions.

By then accounts should have been squared up, borrowed gear returned in good order, and evedybody concerned thanked for their help; more especially of course the owner of the site, who has top priority.

You may have some of his comments to relay to the team, and may have heard the opinions of some of the parents, all of which will help you to come to a fair assessment of the holiday. At this meeting you should try to answer such questions as:

1. Did it achieve its purpose?
2. Did everybody enjoy themselves (including the staff)?
3. Has it improved the unity of the Pack?
4. Was it good publicity for Scouting?
5. What improvements could be made another time?
6. Do you, in fact, ever want to go again?

If the Pack Holiday has really been a success, everybody will want to go again.

These are the notes with which you will conclude your Pack Holiday notebook, and will ensure that next time will be even more successful.

# Recommended Readings

**A.B.C. of Cookery** – (25p) – Her Majesty's Stationery Office.

**Camp Catering and Cooking** – **Rex Hazlewood** – (37½p) – Brown, Son & Ferguson.

**The Camper's Guide from A-Z** – **Rex Hazlewood** – (90p) – Newnes Books Ltd.

**Cub Scout Games** – **Joyce Trimby** – **(50p)** – The Scout Association.

**The Peacock Camping Book** – **Rex Hazlewood and John Thurman** – (17½p) – Penguin.

**The Quartermaster in Camp** – **E. Pleydell-Bouverie** – (10p) – The Girl Guides Association.

**The Scout's Cook Book** – (7½p) – The Scout Association.

**At the time of publishing these books will be available at the prices shown.**

# Index

*Index*

# Notes

# Notes